Mike Daniel's

Frankenstein
The Musical
Libretto

Book, Music and Lyrics

By Mike Daniel

Based on the Novel

By Mary Shelley

Absidy Publishing Company™
Anaheim, CA

For more information about the works of
Mike Daniel, visit http://michaeldaniel.net

List of Characters:

Victor Frankenstein: A young man in his late twenties to mid-thirties. Victor has dark hair, dark eyes, and a ghostly, pale complexion.

Elizabeth Lavenza: Victor's adopted "cousin" and love interest. Elizabeth is in her early twenties.

Henry Clerval: Victor's best friend. A man in his early twenties, Henry is a faithful friend to Victor.

Justine Moritz: William's nanny and faithful friend of the Frankenstein family. Justine should be in her late teens to mid-twenties.

Alphonse Frankenstein: Victor's loving, aging father. Alphonse is a man in his late sixties to early seventies who, despite continuing heart problems, is still "bright of eye."

William Frankenstein[*]**:** Victor's twelve year-old brother.

The Creature[*]**:** Victor's creation. A tall, deformed, yet sympathetic figure driven to murder by the alienation from his father (Victor) and mankind.

DeLacey[*]**:** An old blind man who acquires the friendship of the creature. DeLacey should be in his late sixties to early seventies.

Fritz: A mischievous trouble-making teenager who crosses paths with the Creature. He should be in his early to mid-teens.

The Company: An ensemble of Genevans, mobsters, a Wedding Band (consisting of two fiddles, an alto recorder, double bass and a percussionist) and various incidental roles.

---

[*] These characters have Tenor Recorder solo parts at various points in the show. The orchestra is cued to accommodate if an actor cast in the role is unable to play the part.

Setting:
The action takes place in Geneva, Switzerland in the early 1800's.
Most of the scenes are set in the Frankenstein Chateau.

Victor Frankenstein has recently returned home to Geneva from his studies at Inglestadt. Victor, whose mother, Caroline, died the day he left for Inglestadt, is still crushed by her death. While at Inglestadt, he devoted all of his studies to discovering the secrets of life so that he might be able to "put an end to all death." Now that Victor has returned home, he is putting his knowledge to work to create a living, breathing human being.

Musical Numbers
Prologue
Overture/The Tale of Frankenstein..……COMPANY

Act I
Kyrie Eleison
Scene 1: *Without You*..*Victor, Elizabeth*
I Need Him So...*Elizabeth*
Scene 2: *The Wonders of Nature*..................................*Henry, Victor*
Why, My Lord? (Why Must it End?)..*Victor*
Reflections...*Victor, Henry*
Victor's Dream..*Victor*
Scene 3: *Frankenstein's Opus*..............*Victor, Henry, Elizabeth, ENSEMBLE*
Horrid Wretch...*Victor*
Geneva at Night...*ENSEMBLE*
Scene 4: *At Last a Friend*......................................*DeLacey, Creature*
Scene 5: *No One Can Replace You*..........................*Henry, Justine*
Scene 6: *The Wonders of Knowledge*......................*Creature, Victor*
Awakening...*DeLacey, Creature, Victor*
Fear Not My Friend..*Creature, William*
Don't You Touch Her!...*Henry*
The Curse of Frankenstein..*COMPANY*
Ent'racte

Act II
In Memoria Aeterna

Ent'racte (Optional)
Act II
Requiem

Epilogue *(Optional)*
Pie Jesu

To Mom and Dad,
For putting up with "The Mad Composer" for three long years. It turned out pretty well, didn't it?

Acknowledgements

I would like to thank Bernaldo Evangelista, Loren Wilken, Ken Staton, Chris Roberts, and Gloria Juan for their advice and support in the creation of the score. I would also like to thank Jerry Tracy, Bruce Manaco, Jackie Seaquist, and Luna Edwards for their advice on the libretto. Of course, none of this could have happened without the support of my parents throughout all the endless nights of composing over the three years to write this piece of work. Also, they kind of gave birth to me. All of you helped make this dream come true and I am forever in debt for your generosity.

Prologue
Geneva Graveyard
Midnight

Setting: At C. of the graveyard is a large tombstone marked "Caroline Frankenstein" which is surrounded by dozens of smaller tombstones. U.C. is the Geneva Church, a large, white structure with a cross upon the roof. An operating table hangs from the ceiling, out of the audience's view.

At Rise: *(We open to the sound of the Geneva church bells ringing throughout the darkness. As the bells strike midnight, there is a bolt of lightning[1] and the* Overture *begins. As the lights slowly return, the operating table begins to lower from the ceiling. As the operating table reaches the ground, two GRAVE ROBBERS enter and begin to dig up the grave. They haul a corpse out of the grave and drop it on the operating table. They begin pulling on a pulley system to raise the operating table up to the sky. The GRAVE ROBBERS freeze as there is a bolt of lightning. When the lights return, the stage is empty and the operating table has returned to the ground. The GRAVE ROBBERS poke their heads out from behind the gravestone and look around to make sure that no one is there. Once they're certain that it's safe, they come out and confront the audience.)*

Grave robber 1: *(sings)*
    There is a man named
    Frankenstein!

    Victor Frankenstein!

Grave Robber 2: *(sings)*
    Victor Frankenstein!
    He lives in our town
    Of Geneva!

Both: *(variously)*
    Something is wrong with this man.
    Something's very wrong with
    Victor Frankenstein!

---

[1] Whenever there is a bolt of lightning in the play, the stage is illuminated for a few seconds, then left completely dark.

1

(The church door swings open casting VICTOR FRANKENSTEIN'S shadow across the graveyard and there is a bolt of lightning. When the lights return, the GRAVE ROBBERS are gone, their shovels lying by the grave. The COMPANY is strewn about the stage. A MAN stands in front of the grave.)

Man: *(sings)*
    Now, hear the tale of Frankenstein:
    He was a man who sold his soul
    in hopes that he could
    accomplish his dream,
    his dream of defeating death.
    Victor Frankenstein!

(There is another bolt of lightning and the stage goes dark. There is silence and darkness for a few seconds, then the lights come back up.)

Company: *(sings)*
    Kyrie eleison!
    Christe eleison!
    God please have mercy on us!

(Another bolt of lightning and when the lights return, a small ENSEMBLE stands in front of the grave.)

Man 1: *(sings)*
    Now, hear the tale of his friends:

Woman 1: *(sings)*
    Friends and family.

Woman 2: *(sings)*
    They were all he had in life.

Man 2: *(sings)*
    Victor Frankenstein!

Women:
    But once he—

Men: —sold his soul—

Ensemble:
    —he lost them for sure.
    Victor Frankenstein!

(Another bolt of lightning; through the darkness, we can hear the BASSES chanting "Frankenstein, Frankenstein, Victor Frankenstein."

As the lights come up, the BASSES are raising the operating table by pulling on the pulley system.)

Company: *(sing, variously)*
>Kyrie eleison.
>Christe eleison.
>God please have mercy on us.
>Frankenstein!
>Frankenstein!
>Frankenstein!
>Frankenstein!
>FRANKENSTEIN!!!

(Throughout the chant, the operating table has slowly been rising from the floor to the ceiling. At the end of the chant, it reaches the ceiling and there is a blinding bolt of lightning. From somewhere unseen, the CREATURE roars "FRANKENSTEIN!" When the lights return, the COMPANY has disappeared and VICTOR is standing in front of the grave.)

Victor: *(sings)*
>Now, hear the tale of his monster,
>a deformed and hated wretch,
>who only wished he could be loved
>as he loved his father,
>Victor Frankenstein!

(The COMPANY enters.)

Company: *(sings)*
>Now hear the tale of Frankenstein:
>He was a man who sold his soul—
Women:
>In hopes that he could—
Men: —accomplish his dream—
Company:
>—his dream—
Elizabeth & Victor: *(sing)*
>—of defeating death.

3

Justine and Henry: *(sing)*
    Victor Frankenstein!
Company:
    FRANKENSTEIN!!!

(There is one final burst of lightning and the COMPANY disappears.)

Blackout.

Interlude

(A small semicircle of VICTOR'S friends and family appear in a spotlight, with WILLIAM at the center of the circle. ALPHONSE steps forward.)

Alphonse: *(music under)* Victor was never the same after Caroline died...*I* was never the same. The day after she died, he left to pursue his studies in the natural sciences at Inglestadt. He returned home one year ago, but he wasn't the same Victor I had watched grow up. He was distant—distracted. *(Indicating WILLIAM)* Poor William grew to be quite scared of his older brother.

(ALPHONSE disappears into the darkness. JUSTINE steps forward.)

Justine: *(music under)* I never knew Madame Caroline. I was hired to take care of poor William after she died. No one knew what it was that killed her, which made it all the more hard for the dear Frankensteins, the kindest people I've ever had the pleasure to work for.

(JUSTINE disappears into the darkness and HENRY steps forward.)

Henry: *(music under)* Victor kept to himself, even before his mother died. I was a few years behind Victor in my studies at Inglestadt, but when I received a letter from Alphonse asking me to return home for Victor's sake as soon as possible, I left immediately.

(HENRY disappears into the darkness and ELIZABETH steps forward.)

4

Elizabeth: *(music under)* Victor and I grew up together. First in two different households, then—after my father died—in one. Even so, we never thought of each other as brother and sister, just the best of friends…maybe more. You could never be entirely sure with Victor.

(ELIZABETH disappears into the darkness, leaving WILLIAM alone in the spotlight.)

Blackout.
Music Continues Under Scene Change if Necessary.
End of Prologue.

Act I
Scene I
Frankenstein Chateau Living Room
Late Afternoon

Setting: The living room consists of a couch, chairs, and a coffee table. At R., there is a fireplace with a picture of a beautiful woman on the mantle. The hallway door leading into the living room is U.C. At L. is a door leading to an unseen stair case leading to VICTOR's lab.

At Rise: *(ELIZABETH enters through the U.C. door with ALPHONSE. Music plays and fades under the scene.)*

Alphonse: Henry will be arriving from Inglestadt later this evening, Elizabeth, but I was hoping you might have a word with Victor first. I hate to make it seem as if we're taking sides against him like this, but we need to make sure that he realizes that we're concerned about him.

Elizabeth: I completely agree, Alphonse. Victor and I were so close before his mother died, now we barely even see each other.

Alphonse: *(Bursting out.)* It's those damned experiments of his! *(Blushing over his outburst.)* Forgive me, Elizabeth. I just hate to see my son throw his life away over silly experiments.

Elizabeth: We all do, Alphonse. Don't worry, Henry and I will talk to him and we'll help him get through this. Everything will turn out fine.

Alphonse: Thank you, Elizabeth.

(ALPHONSE kisses her lightly on the cheek and exits through the U.C. door. ELIZABETH takes a deep breath and knocks on the R. door.)

Victor's Voice: *(calling from upstairs)* Who is it?

Elizabeth: Victor, it's me, Elizabeth. We need to talk.

Victor: I'm too busy, come back later.

Elizabeth: Victor, we *need* to talk.

(Footsteps can be heard descending a staircase and VICTOR emerges from his lab. ELIZABETH, startled to see his pale complexion, gasps.)

Elizabeth: Victor, what has happened to you?

Victor: What do you mean?

Elizabeth: Just look at you, you're a wreck! What happened to the Victor I used to know? My father would be ashamed to see you like this.

Victor: He couldn't have had such high hopes for me at such a young age.

Elizabeth: Why are you always like this? Ever since you came back from Inglestadt you've been so...standoffish. *(VICTOR remains frozen, emotionless.)* If not for my father's sake, then for your mother's! Please just—

Victor: *(lashing out)* For God's sake, Elizabeth, let me be!

(ELIZABETH stares, hurt and near tears, at VICTOR.)

Elizabeth: What's happened to you? What's happened to *us?*

(VICTOR, stunned by her question, crosses to her and places a comforting hand on her shoulder.)

Victor: *(sings)*
       For five years I've faced the world alone.
       I've spent those years pursuing my dreams.
       My elders told me I was
       wasting my time;
       That dreamers are losers;
       That I should not
       Throw my life away.

       But now my dreams are starting to come true.

The past five years are coming into play.
The day will soon be here when
 I will prove them wrong.
But it will mean nothing
if I cannot
share the dream with you.

My life is empty without you.
Without you, the morning sun does not rise.
I can't bare the thought of life without you.
Without you, I could not go on.

(ELIZABETH takes his hand and leads him to the couch, where they sit.)

Elizabeth: *(sings)*
I wish you'd let me into your world.
I long so much to know what's on your mind.
I love you so much!
Please don't lock me out!
My life is so empty
if I cannot share it with you.
My life is empty without you.

Together: *(sing)*
Without you!
I long so much to be by your side.
It's all too clear that we are meant to be.
My life is worth living
now that you're hear with me!
My life is worth nothing
if I cannot share it with you.
My life is empty without you!
My life's empty without you!

(They begin to kiss, the break away, embarrassed.)

Victor: *(music under)* Elizabeth, you have nothing to fear. Soon you will see no more of this tired, wretched Victor Frankenstein—only the loving, caring Victor you once knew. I promise.

Elizabeth: *(music under)* Victor, it's just that we're all scared for you. It's not healthy to lock yourself inside that lab all day and night.

Victor: Elizabeth, my experiments will be finished by the end of the week, I promise you.

Elizabeth: You promise?

Victor: I promise on all my heart and soul. On Saturday, when this is all over and done, we'll go out and have a nice quiet picnic, just you and me. Like old times. Is it a date?

Elizabeth: It's a date.

(VICTOR kisses her lightly on the cheek and returns to his lab. ELIZABETH sits on the couch, pondering.)

Elizabeth: *(sings)*
>I've always been there for him
>through the good and the bad.
>But he's not here when I need him
>most of all in my empty life.
>Doesn't he love me?

(Rising off the couch.)
>I should leave him in darkness
>as he's done to me.
>I am alone without him here.
>Why can't I just leave him all alone?
>
>There was a time, so very long ago,
>when nothing came between us.
>But now those days have died
>and he's not here for me!
>
>I need him in my life.
>I'm incomplete without him.
>I can't go on without his smile.
>To light my day, I will stand by him

9

through good and bad.
I need him so.
(Sitting back on the couch.)
I love him so.

Blackout.
End of Scene I.

Act I
Scene II
Frankenstein Chateau
Later That Evening

At Rise: *(ELIZABETH is pacing around impatiently in the living room. WILLIAM and JUSTINE are sitting on the couch looking at a picture book while ALPHONSE is sitting in his rocking chair smoking his pipe. There is a knock on the door. Music plays and fades under the scene)*

Elizabeth: *(as she eagerly runs for the door)* Justine, could you put William to bed, please?

Justine: *(rising)* Of course.

William: Elizabeth, I'm almost eleven! I don't have to go to bed early anymore.

Elizabeth: *(snapping)* William, just go!

Justine: *(comforting WILLIAM who stares, hurt, at ELIZABETH)* Come along William. You don't want to be awake when your brother comes downstairs all grumpy from working all night on his experiments, do you? *(Looking at ELIZABETH, who ignores her.)* Then you'll have two crabs yelling at you.

William: *(regretfully rising)* All right.

(WILLIAM hesitates, then JUSTINE takes his hand and leads him to the U.C. door. As she opens the door, HENRY enters. JUSTINE and HENRY make eye contact for a few seconds, then WILLIAM tugs on her skirt and brings them out of their trance.)

Henry: *(clearing his throat, awkwardly)* Good to see you, Justine.

Justine: *(blushing as she carries WILLIAM off to bed)* Same to you, Henry.

11

(JUSTINE exits with WILLIAM as HENRY crosses C. and hugs ELIZABETH. ALPHONSE rises to greet HENRY.)

Henry: *(embracing ELIZABETH)* Dearest Elizabeth!

Elizabeth: Henry, thank you for coming.

Alphonse: *(shaking HENRY'S hand)* Good to see you Henry. How are your studies at Inglestadt?

Henry: They're going well, Alphonse. *(noticing ALPHONSE'S weak appearance)* Is your heart still giving you trouble?

Alphonse: *(obviously holding back)* Not as much as when Caroline died, *(crosses himself)* God bless her soul.

Elizabeth: Henry, we're sorry for dragging you away from your studies on such short notice, it's just that Victor…hasn't been himself since he came home.

Henry: What exactly is wrong with Victor, Elizabeth?

Elizabeth: Frankly, I don't know what's wrong with him. He just hasn't been the same since his mother died. He locks himself inside his lab and stays there all day and night. We barely even know him now.

Alphonse: Henry, we were hoping that maybe you could help him through these hard times.

Henry: Fear not my friends, I'll talk to him. If I can't help him then no one can. *(VICTOR'S footsteps can be heard descending the staircase.)* Quick, I think I hear him coming down now! It would be best if you leave us alone to catch up on old times.

Elizabeth: *(leaving)* Thank you, Henry.

Alphonse: *(leading ELIZABETH out the U.C. door)* Come, Elizabeth.

(As ALPHONSE and ELIZABETH exit, VICTOR enters through the R. door.)

12

Henry: Long time no see, Victor Frankenstein.

(VICTOR, surprised to see his best friend, rushes to HENRY and embraces him.)

Victor: Henry Clerval?! A very long time indeed! What brings you to Geneva old friend?

(HENRY hesitates a moment, then decides to tell VICTOR why he came.)

Henry: *(music under)* Victor, I have to confess. Your family brought me here today. Victor, they're very concerned about your studies. *(VICTOR remains unresponsive.)* Victor, listen to me! Elizabeth and Alphonse are extremely concerned.

(VICTOR stares at HENRY coldly for a second, then shrugs it off with a nervous laugh, turning his back to HENRY.)

Victor: *(music under)* They need not worry.

Henry: *(crossing to VICTOR, sings)*
  Victor seeing you now,
  pale as a ghost,
  makes me believe that they do.
  Victor, please tell me
  about your studies
  that have plagued your soul.

Victor: *(turning his back on HENRY again, speaks, music under)* You would never understand.

Henry: *(speaks, music under)* Try me.

(VICTOR suddenly turns on HENRY, scaring him back)
Victor: *(sings)*
  You can never dream
  the wonders I've discovered.
  From the basics of chemistry

to the anatomy of the human body.
Nature is amazing!

I cannot describe to you
the wonders I've discovered.
From the origins of nature
to the secrets of life itself!

(VICTOR suddenly becomes tense as he looks back on the painful memory)
I have vowed on my mother's deathbed
I would avenge her death by hunting down death!
I vowed I would hunt Death down to my own death!
Now, on this day that I've found Death, he had better pray!
For, on this day that I've found Death, this day will be his last!

(VICTOR breaks down, near tears, and falls to his knees)

Why, my lord, why must it end?
Why do you have to put us through such pain?
Why must we feel the pain of losing our loved ones?
(rises, reaching out toward the sky)
Why, my Lord, must it end?
(falling down)
Why can't it just go on and on?

(VICTOR rises and begins pacing around impatiently, talking and pointing at the sky)
Tell me God,
why must life end so suddenly?
Why can't we just
continue on without losing our loved ones?

Tell me God,
why must we go through so much pain?
Why can't we just
go through life without feeling remorse?
Tell me God!

(VICTOR crumbles back to his knees)

14

Why, my Lord, why must it end?
Why do you have to put us through such pain?
Why must we feel the pain of losing our loved ones?
(rising again)
Why, my Lord,must it end?
(falling to his knees again)
Why can't it just go on and on?

(VICTOR crumples into a ball on the floor. HENRY moves over to his friend to comfort him.)

Henry: *(placing a hand on VICTOR'S shoulder)* Victor...

Victor: *(lashing out)* What?!

(VICTOR, realizing he lost control of himself, suddenly regains his composure and rises to apologize to his friend.)

Victor: *(sings)*
I'm so sorry, my dear Henry,
for making your return so gloomy.
Let us celebrate this happy occasion
with the best of news.

(VICTOR reaches into his coat pocket and pulls out a large engagement ring. HENRY stares at it, in awe, for a few seconds.)
I remember the day that my
parents brought Elizabeth to our home.
An orphan at the age of six,
she was the saddest child in the world.
But I looked past those sad eyes
and saw the most beautiful
diamonds in the known world.
I knew that she was, and always would be mine.

(HENRY, overjoyed, grasps his friend's hand and pats him on the back, congratulating him.)

Henry: *(sings)*
Victor this certainly is the best of news!

15

I could not be happier for the two of you!
But I fear it would be worst
if you were to marry her while
you're so lost in your studies.

Victor: *(sings)*
      Henry don't worry, I will not marry her
      until I'm done with my experiments.
Both: Until that day Until that day when—
Victor:
      —she will be mine!
Henry: *(sings)*
      When she will be yours!
Both: It would be best to wait for that
      joyous day!

(HENRY shakes VICTOR'S hand again.)

Henry: So, when are you planning to propose.

Victor: *(looking at the R. door)* As soon as I'm done with my experiments.

(There is a distant roll of thunder. HENRY stares, troubled, at VICTOR for a few moments, then extends his hand to VICTOR.)

Henry: Well, Victor, I guess I had better go bring my luggage in. It sounds like there will be rain tonight.

Victor: Yes…

Henry: I'll leave you alone now.

Victor: *(taking HENRY'S hand)* It's good to see you again, Henry. Tell Elizabeth and father that I shall be ready for dinner in an hour or so.

(HENRY nods his head and exits through the U.C. door. VICTOR watches HENRY leave and steps into a spotlight as the lights go dead.)

Interlude

Victor: *(music under)* If I were to create a man—yes, if I were to create a man—would it then not be possible to put an end to all death?
(sings)
Families would suffer no more;
Lovers would never separate;
And no one would ever separate;
And no one would ever again feel
The pain that has become my life.
(speaks, music under) Are these not noble intentions? If putting my friends and family on hold is the price to pay, then I will gladly pay it so that
(sings)
families will suffer no more;
Lovers will never separate;
And no one will ever again feel
the pain that has become my life.
(speaks, music under)
After all, my friends and family will still be here when all is said and done...won't they?

(VICTOR disappears into the darkness and a GENEVAN WOMAN steps forward out of the darkness.)

Woman: *(music under)* Rumors started going around about what was going on under the Frankenstein roof. The townspeople talked often, as townspeople often do. Some claimed Victor was meddling with witchcraft. The more educated townsmen said he was trying to make himself God. I personally just thought he was insane.

(The WOMAN steps out of the light. A GENEVAN MAN steps forward.)

Man: *(music under)* I never knew the Frankensteins. They never had the time of day for a commoner such as myself. But I knew that something not right was going on in that house. Something not right at all.

17

(The MAN steps out of the light.)

Blackout.
Music Continues Under Remaining Scene Change if Necessary.
End of Scene II.

Act I
Scene III
Victor's Lab
Later That Night

Setting: Victor's lab is a large set, containing several machines, a desk with a chair at D.C., and an operating table at C. with a body on it. The body is covered by white cloth. D.R. is a door leading to the staircase to the living room. D.L. is a large mirror. U.C. is a large window through which the audience can see out into the stormy night. Beside the window is a couch which VICTOR sleeps on.

At Rise: *(A bolt of lightning lights up the scene. VICTOR is working hastily at his experiment table, mixing chemicals and other strange experiments.)*

Victor: *(sings)*
>All these tests!
>All these experiments!
>I can't believe my mind!
>Everything is suddenly
>fitting into place!
>All my dreams, and my fantasies
>suddenly coming true!

(keening)
>But if only I could have saved
>my dear mother from her death,
>my life would not be so empty!

(Gaining control, VICTOR scolds himself for getting off track.)
>Stop it!
>I will never finish my experiments

18

if I keep dwelling on what's dead and gone!

(There's another bolt of lightning and VICTOR looks out the window into the storm. He then begins running around hooking up the equipment and preparing for the experiment.)
>All these machines!
>All this equipment!
>
>I can't believe myself!
>I can feel the end of death
>right within my grasp!
>All my dreams, and my fantasies
>suddenly coming true!

(keening again)
>And I promise to my loved ones
>I will never ever let harm come to you!

(scolding himself)
>Stop it!

(Two GENEVANS appear at either side of the stage.)

Genevan 1: *(sings)*
>And he will do his best
>to save their lives—

Genevan 2: *(sings)*
>--but his fam'ly's fate   Genevan 1:
>Lies in God's own hands!   God's own hands!

(HENRY and ELIZABETH approach the D.R. from the "stair case" as the GENEVANS start chanting "Frankenstein, Frankenstein, Victor Frankenstein" variously.)

Henry: *(pounding on door, sings)*
>Victor open up!   Elizabeth: *(sings)*
>   Victor please, let us in!

(VICTOR starts hooking machinery up to the body on the operating table and starts to raise the table up to the ceiling.)

Victor: *(sings)*
> It is here!
> The time has come!
> I can't believe my eyes!
> All my dreams are coming true
> right before my eyes!
> All my dreams and my fantasies
> suddenly coming true!

Henry: *(sings, simultaneously with above)*	Elizabeth: *(sings)*
Victor why won't you let us in?	Victor please, let us in!
Victor open this door I say!	Victor please, open the door!
Victor this is insane!	Victor please let us help you!
Let us in!	Let us in!
Why won't you let us help you?	Victor please let us help you!
Victor, open up!	Victor, please, let us in!

Victor, Elizabeth, & Genevans:	Henry:
All my/your/his dreams!	Open this door!
All my/your/his fantasies!	Listen to me Frankenstein!

(Now the operating table has reached the ceiling and rests as VICTOR looks up at it in awe.)
Victor:
> Suddenly coming true!

Elizabeth, Henry & Genevans:
> FRANKENSTEIN!!!

(A bolt of lightning strikes and the machinery in VICTOR'S lab lights up. ELIZABETH and HENRY freeze, stunned by the unexpected explosion. The GENEVANS disappear. When the lights return to normal, the scene focuses on VICTOR. VICTOR lowers the operating

table and lifts the CREATURE'S arm, searching for a pulse. As he feels none, he disappointedly drops the arm, moves over to his desk and starts to write in his journal.)

Victor: *(sings)*
> For five years I've faced the world alone.
> I've spent five years pursuing my dreams.
> My elders told me I was
> wasting my time;
> That dreamers are losers.
> And now I fear
> I see that they were right for
> tonight my tests have ended.
> The experiment was a failure.
> My creation lies dead as it ever was.
> I am ashamed of myself.

(VICTOR closes the journal, places it in his coat pocket and heads to the D.R. door. He opens the door to find ELIZABETH and HENRY waiting eagerly for him and lets them into his lab.)

Victor: It's over. The experiment was a failure.

Henry: *(comforting VICTOR)* Victor, it's all right. Maybe it's for the best.

(VICTOR, oblivious to HENRY'S words, tosses his coat on the chair at the desk, crosses U.C. and collapses onto the bed.)

Henry: Victor, it's time to move—

(ELIZABETH cuts him off by placing her hand on his arm and raising a finger to her mouth for silence.)

Elizabeth: Just let him be alone for a while.

(HENRY begins to protest, but ELIZABETH leads him out. As VICTOR falls asleep, the CREATURE can be seen slowly sitting up on the operating table. He stands up and begins staggering around the room, getting in touch with his senses. He then makes his way over to the

mirror and jumps, startled to see the reflection in the mirror. He shakes his hand at the reflection trying to shoo it away, and when it imitates him, he stares at it, offended. When he sees the reflection stare back at him, too, he realizes that it must be a "copy" of himself. He feels his face, disgusted by the ugliness caused by the stitches covering it. Noticing VICTOR on the bed, the CREATURE slowly walks over to the bed and places a hand on VICTOR'S shoulder. As VICTOR begins to stir, the CREATURE tries to speak, but only utters inarticulate moans. VICTOR groggily opens his eyes, then jumps up, startling the CREATURE. He then begins shouting at the CREATURE, with every shout, the CREATURE winces in pain.)

Victor: *(sings)*
> Fiend!
> Get out of my house,
> you horrid wretch!
> What the Hell was I thinking
> creating such a monster?
> Beast!
> What was I thinking?
> You're a horrid wretch!
> Get out of my house you fiend
> and bother me no more!

(VICTOR grabs his coat from the chair and throws it at the CREATURE who grabs it and, crying, jumps through the U.C. window, causing it to shatter. VICTOR runs to the window and looks out into the dark and stormy night as HENRY and ELIZABETH run into the room to see what all the commotion was about.)

Henry: Victor, what's the matter? We heard screaming!

Victor: *(breathing deeply)* I…just had a bad dream is all.

Elizabeth: *(looking at the broken window)* Victor, why is the window broken?

Victor: *(stumbling to come up with an excuse)* I…must have thrown something in my sleep. *(He looks at the tipped over chair where his coat was and realizes that his journal was inside.)* My journal! It has

22

my jour… *(catching himself)* I mean…I must have thrown my coat in my sleep. My journal was inside my coat. That must be why the window's broken.

(HENRY crosses U.C. and looks out into the dark, trying to see if VICTOR'S coat is on the ground below.)

Henry: Victor, I can't see your coat, or anything else that you might have thrown.

(As VICTOR tries to come up with something to say, HENRY notices something on the windowsill and wipes his finger across the sill. HENRY looks at his finger and then walks back into the room and holds out his finger for VICTOR to look at.)

Henry: Victor, there's blood on the windowsill.

(VICTOR stares at the blood on HENRY'S finger for a few seconds, stumbles and faints to the ground. As the lights dim out, ELIZABETH and HENRY run to VICTOR'S unconscious body.)

Blackout.

Interlude

(A light comes up on VICTOR.)

Victor: *(music under)* That night I fell into a serious brain fever that would last over a year. I had no way to warn the town that a demon was running loose. The best I could hope for would be that the creature would die from starvation or some such fate of nature. Unfortunately, fate had its own plans…

(An ENSEMBLE steps into the spotlight as VICTOR steps out.)
Ensemble: *(sings)*
    Geneva at night
    is not a place to be
    'cause in Geneva at night
    your mind makes you see
    what you don't.

23

Keep your children inside
in Geneva at night.

(The CREATURE, confused and lost, runs into the spotlight, only to be met by the hateful shouts of the ENSEMBLE.)
Ensemble: *(variously)*
Beast!
Fiend!
Get out of our town,
you horrid wretch!

(Terrified, the CREATURE retreats back into the darkness.)

Various Soloists: *(sing)*
Have you ever
Looked Death in the eye?
Well, in Geneva at night
you will shake hands
with Satan himself.
Try to stay off the streets
of Geneva at night!

(Once again, the CREATURE stumbles into the spotlight only to be chased away by the ENSEMBLE.)
Ensemble: *(variously)*
Beast!
Fiend!
Get away from us,
you horrid wretch!

Various Soloists:
Do you feel empty
without your reality?
Well, then in Geneva at night,
you had better get out of town
'cause in Geneva at night,
there's no reality.

(One final time, the CREATURE stumbles into the wrong place at the wrong time and is chased off by the ENSEMBLE.)

Ensemble: *(variously)*
>Beast!
>Fiend!
>Why won't you go away,
>you horrid wretch?
>FRANKENSTEIN!

(ENSEMBLE chants "Frankenstein, Frankenstein, Victor Franken-stein!" variously.)
Solo: *(sings)*
>Frankenstein was a man who
>sold his soul to the Devil.
>Everything that Victor did
>was well-meaning
>but in the end
>the darkness
>took control!
>Frakenstein!

Blackout.
End of Scene III.

Act I
Scene IV
DeLacey's Hut
The Next Morning

Setting: The hut is a small set, almost empty on the inside except for a chair, a bed, and a fireplace.

At Rise: *(The CREATURE stumbles through the woods, crying and falls to the ground in front of the hut. Inside of the hut, DELACEY picks up his recorder and begins playing. The CREATURE rises, appeased by the lovely music, and enters the hut in search of its source. Hearing someone enter, DELACEY jumps up startled.)*

DeLacey: *(sings)*
> Who is there?
> *(speaks, music under)*
For once could you rotten kids leave me alone?

(The CREATURE, not knowing how to reply, only repeats DELACEY'S question.)

Creature: *(sings)*
> WHO IS THERE?

DeLacey: *(speaks, music under)* Oh, so you're a comedian now, eh? Well, I don't find it funny.

Creature: *(sings)*
> FUNNY?

DeLacey: *(sings)*
> What's wrong with you,
> can't you speak?

Creature: *(sings)*
> SPEAK?

DeLacey: *(believing he understands, sings)*
    Oh, now I see.
(speaks) You're some poor retarded man, aren't you? Come in, come in. Warm yourself by the fire. I can't offer you much. But what I can offer is yours.

(The CREATURE slowly enters and DELACEY leads him to a chair.)

DeLacey: So, what happened to you, you poor man? *(Realizing his mistake.)* Never mind, don't bother answering. My name is DeLacey. Can you say that? De-La-cey?

Creature: DE…LA…CEY.

DeLacey: Well, you seem to be very good about repeating, so try this. Just repeat everything I say, okay?

(The CREATURE stares blankly at him.)

DeLacey: Hmm…well, just repeat what I say even if you don't understand me.
    (sings)
    A, B, C, D, E, F, G…
    (speaks)
Now you try. Go ahead.

Creature: *(sings)*
    A…B…C…D…E…F…G…

DeLacey: *(speaks)* Very good. You know, for a dumb fellow you sure are smart. I don't how you became dumb, but I'll help you. I'll be your teacher…and friend.

(DELACEY slowly walks D.C. while the CREATURE watches him.)

DeLacey: *(sings)*
    At last a friend!
    I've waited so long.
    I've been so alone
    all of these years!

27

But now, you're here
and my emptiness is gone.
For now I have a friend.

(Taking the hesitant CREATURE by the hand.)
Come here my friend.
Please don't worry.
I would not dream
of hurting my friend,
my one and only friend.
Now I have a friend.

(Becoming more excited.)
Listen my friend,
I'll be your teacher.
I'll teach you about
all of your dreams!
I may be blind,
but I still can teach you
all the world.
My dearest friend.
Finally a friend!

Creature: *(speaks, music under)* FRIEND?

DeLacey: *(taking the CREATURE'S hand)* Yes, friend.

Interlude

(As the lights go dead, VICTOR enters into a D.R. spotlight.)
Victor: *(music under)* Over the next year, while I was recovering from my brain fever, my family was left unwarned of the storm that was brewing—and would soon approach.

(VICTOR disappears into the darkness.)
Blackout.
End of Scene IV.

Act I
Scene V
The Woods
Ten Months Later

Setting: Very simple set, no buildings, just trees, stumps.

At Rise: *(JUSTINE, HENRY and WILLIAM are having a picnic in the woods. JUSTINE and HENRY are sitting close together on a blanket. WILLIAM is sitting on a nearby stump playing his recorder.)*

Justine: William, why don't you run off and play your recorder somewhere else?

William: *(rising)* Okay. *(hesitating)* You two aren't gonna kiss like you did the last time I left you alone, are ya?

Justine: *(blushing)* No, now go run off.

William: *(reluctantly)* Okay. *(WILLIAM exits U.R.)*

Justine: *(moving closer to HENRY)* Henry, I'm so worried about Victor. He's been sick for so long now.

Henry: *(comforting her)* Justine, please don't worry. Victor will be fine. He's always been a survivor.

Justine: *(blushing)* Henry, I'm so sorry. Look at me, I'm a nervous wreck! *(Grasping the necklace around her neck that's carrying an engagement ring.)* It's no wonder you don't want to tell the Frankenstein's about our engagement. What could you possibly see in me?

(HENRY rises and proclaims his love to the world.)

Henry: *(sings)*
> I see the stars in your eyes.
> I see angels in your face.
> But above all, I see you.

29

I see roses in your cheeks.
I see rainbows in your smile.
But above all this,
yes, above all this,
I see you.
You and only you.
Wonderful, beautiful you.

(HENRY gets down on one knee, takes her hands in his and looks her in the eyes.)

No one can replace you,
no one can compare.
No one will replace you,
no one will come close.

Of all the women in the world
none compare to you, my dear!
No one can replace you,
no one can compare.

(HENRY rises, holding JUSTINE'S hands and she rises with him.)

Justine: *(sings)*

When I'm around you, my love,
I feel as if I can fly!
All because I love you.
I have never in my life
met such a man who moves me so.
But above all this,
yes, above all this,
I love you.
You and only you.
Wonderful, charming you.

(They lower onto their knees, inches away from each other.)

No one can make me
feel the way you do.
No one can come close
to replacing you.
Of all the men in the world
none compare to you, my love.

No one can replace you,
no one can compare.

Together:
No one can replace you,
no one can compare.
Nothing can compare to
the way I feel with you.

Henry: *(rising)*
Others will try to replace your smile—
that precious smile—
but in the end—

(HENRY lowers back down to eye level.)
Together:
No one can replace you,
no one can compare.

(They kiss. WILLIAM enters U.R.)

William: Aww…you said you weren't gonna kiss.

Interlude
(As the lights fade out, VICTOR walks into a D.R. spotlight.)

Victor: Over the next year, while my family was taking care of me, my creation made extraordinary progress unlike anything I could have ever dreamed…or dread.

Blackout.
End of Scene V.

Act I
Scene VI
DeLacey's Hut
Twighlight; A Little Later

At Rise: *(DELACEY is sleeping in the hut, snoring lightly.)*

Creature: *(whispering to the snoozing DELACEY)* Rest, my friend, the sun is dipping below the horizon. I shall not wander far.

(The CREATURE steps out of the hut and takes a stroll through the woods. He pulls out his recorder and begins playing as he walks. He stops playing and confronts the audience.)

Creature: *(sings)*
> You can never dream
> the wonders I've discovered!
> From the simple ABC's
> to reading the Christian Bible.
> Knowledge is amazing!

(The CREATURE begins to play his recorder again, then stops to confront the audience again.)

> You can never ever dream,
> the knowledge I've discovered!
> From the simplest of lit'rature
> to Milton's Paradise Lost!

(pondering)
> But I have often wondered
> who is my father, my mother?
> Surely there must be someone out there,
> someone who brought me into this life.
> Am I alone in this cruel world
> with no parents to comfort me?

(The CREATURE stops as he has a flashback from the night of his "birth.")

Victor's Voice: *(sings)*
>Fiend!
>Get out of my house, you fiend!
>And bother me no more!

(The CREATURE tenses up, then shivers and shakes it off. He sits down on a log and begins to play his recorder again. As he plays, FRITZ creeps into the scene carrying a lantern, apparently planning to rob DELACEY. However, as he enters the hut, he notices the CREATURE and freezes, dropping the lantern into the door of the hut.)

Fritz: *(whispers, music under)* Holy shit!

(Behind him, smoke has begun to rise out of the hut. The smell of the smoke makes its way to the CREATURE who suddenly stops playing and rises. When he sees FRITZ by the hut, he runs, screaming, at him.)

Creature: *(music under)* What are you doing? Get away!

(FRITZ, terrified, scrambles off into the woods screaming. The CREATURE watches after him for a few seconds, not noticing that smoke is pouring out of the hut and flames can be seen from within. Suddenly DELACEY'S scream pierces the air. Screaming, the CREATURE runs into the hut. He emerges seconds later, coughing, and carrying DELACEY'S limp body in his arms.)

Creature: *(sobbing, music under)* Live! Please live! Don't leave me, DeLacey!

(An ENSEMBLE appears and accompanies/chants as DELACEY suddenly springs into consciousness and grabs the CREATURE around the collar.)

DeLacey: *(gasping for air, sings)*
>Friend, I see a storm approaching you.
>Take this warning and listen good.
>A curse lies on the house of Frankenstein!
>Beware the house of Victor Frankenstein!

33

(With that, DELACEY goes limp. The CREATURE lets out a howl of pain, clutching DELACEY'S dead body close to him.)

Creature: *(sings)*
> Why, my Lord, why must it end?
> Why do you have to put us through such pain?
> Why can't it just go on and on?
> Why did you have to take DeLacey away from me?
(tensing as he rises)
> Why, my Lord, must it end?
(falling back down to DELACEY'S corpse)
> Why can't it just go on and on?

(The CREATURE rises and begins pacing.)
> Tell me God,
> why must life end so suddenly?
> Why can't I just
> continue on without losing my dear friend?
>
> Tell me God,
> why must I go through so much pain?
> Why can't I just
> go through life without feeling remorse?
> Tell me God!!!

(As the CREATURE thrusts his fist into the air, VICTOR'S journal falls out of his coat pocket—which the CREATURE has kept from the night of his "birth"—and onto the ground. The CREATURE bends down to pick it up and begins to read the dedication page.)

Creature: *(sings, reading)*
> "This is the journal of Frankenstein…"

(The CREATURE begins to skim through the book.)
> "…I simply cannot explain
> the wonders I've discovered—"

Victor's Voice: *(taking over, sings)*
> "—I have set out to create

a living and breathing human being!
Nature is amazing…!"

(The CREATURE turns to another page.)
V.V.: "…I cannot believe myself!
It is finally almost done!
It is truly amazing
to create a human being!
I cannot believe myself…!"

(The CREATURE turns to the last page in the book.)
V.V.: "…Tonight my tests have ended.
The experiment was a failure.
My creation lies dead as it ever was…"

Creature: *(taking over, sings)*
"…I am ashamed of myself…"

(CREATURE falls to his knees and drops the journal on the ground, stunned at the realization that he is not human.)

Creature: *(sings)*
Oh, my God, I'm not human!
I do not have a mother or a father—
I do not have a God!
(tensing as he rises)
Oh, my God!
What the Hell am I?
(falling back to his knees)
I'm not human nor animal!

(VICTOR'S words from the night of the "birth" come back into CREATURE'S memory.)

Victor's Voice: *(sings)*
Fiend!
Get out of my house!
You horrid wretch!

(CREATURE, becoming furious, rises and screams into the woods.)

Creature: *(sings)*
> FRANKENSTEIN!!!
> Here, today, I swear with God as my witness,
> I will dedicate my life to hunting down this Frankenstein!
> I vow I will hunt him down to my own death!
> And on the day that I find him, he had better pray!
> For on the day that I find him, that day will be his last!

(ENSEMBLE disappears. Suddenly, recorder music can be heard playing in the woods.)

Creature: *(music under)* DeLacey? Is that you, old friend?

(WILLIAM enters from R., to the disappointment of CREATURE, and jumps, startled by seeing CREATURE. He then sees the burned hut and DELACEY'S body and screams out for help.)

William: *(music under)* Justine! Justine! Help me! It's a monster!

(CREATURE runs to WILLIAM, trying to quiet him.)

Creature: Shh! Quiet boy! I won't hurt you!

William: *(whimpering)* If you even touch me, my father will make you very sorry that you did.

Creature: Who is your father?

William: Alphonse Frankenstein… Help! Somebody help me!

Creature: *(cursing under his breath, music sting under)* Frankenstein!

(CREATURE slowly creeps toward the screaming WILLIAM then, suddenly, becomes gentle again.)

Creature: Tell me boy, what is that pendant around your neck?

William: *(warily)* It's a picture of my mother, Caroline Frankenstein. The prettiest lady in all of Geneva…until she died that is.

Creature: *(chuckling lightly)* How sweet. May I look at it?

(WILLIAM backs away.)

Creature: Oh come on, you're not still scared of me, are you? I was just strolling through the woods when I came across the hut. *(bitterly)* I tried to save the old man, but I couldn't.

(When CREATURE sees that WILLIAM still hasn't relaxed, he sits down on a log and indicates for WILLIAM to sit down next to him. WILLIAM remains standing.)

Creature: *(sings)*
>Fear not my friend,
>please do not worry.
>I would not dream
>of hurting you, my friend!
>My little friend,
>my one and only friend.
>Fear not my friend.

(Indicating for WILLIAM to sit, which he does, cautiously.)
>Sit here my friend.
>You need not worry.
>I could not hurt
>such an innocent child!
>My little friend,
>my one and only friend.
>Fear not my friend.

William: *(warily, sings)*
>You say you're my friend,
>then why do I fear you?
>I'm scared to trust
>such an ugly monster!
>My scary friend.
>Why am I so scared?
>I'm scared my friend.

Creature:	William:
Fear not my friend,	I'm scared
I could not hurt you.	my friend.
Come here and let me	This feels
look at your locket.	so wrong.
My little friend,	Why am
my one and only friend.	I scared?
	I'm so scared.
Come here my friend.	
	Why am I scared?
Fear not my friend.	
Fear not my friend!!!	I'm scared my—

(WILLIAM allows CREATURE to see his locket and CREATURE grabs WILLIAM by the throat and strangles him to death, ripping the locket from WILLIAM'S neck in the process.)

Creature: *(realizing what he has done)* What have I done? Oh, no! What have I done? I can't stay here!

(He runs off L. The hut disappears and we see HENRY and JUSTINE sleeping in the woods. CREATURE runs on from L. and sees them, pained by their happiness.)

Creature: Look at them—so happy. What do they have which makes them worthy of happiness and love that I have not? Am I so wretched a being that I cannot be loved as they love?

(He kneels by JUSTINE'S sleeping body and begins stroking her hair.)

Creature: Shall I never know the caress of such a beautiful creature?

(JUSTINE awakens and begins screaming when she sees CREATURE. CREATURE rises to quiet her.)

Creature: *(music under)* Quiet, girl! I mean you no harm.

(HENRY awakens. When he sees CREATURE, he jumps in front of JUSTINE, protecting her.)

Henry: *(sings)*
>Don't you touch her!
>Don't you touch her!
>I swear on father's grave
>that if you touch her
>the house of Frankenstein

(CREATURE tenses and slowly makes his way toward them)
>will have a bounty on your head
>quicker than you can blink.
>Don't you touch her!
>Don't you touch her!

(backing away as CREATURE approaches them)
>Don't you touch her!

Creature: *(under his breath, music under)* Frankenstein. *(to JUSTINE and HENRY)* So, you belong to the house of Frankenstein? Then I have a present for your master, Victor. *(Throwing WILLIAM'S locket at JUSTINE)* Give that to your master Frankenstein and tell him of the curse that rests on his house and everyone in it! Go! Go and tell master Frankenstein! *(JUSTINE and HENRY, frozen with fear, don't move)* Go, I say GO!!!

(As JUSTINE and HENRY run away, lightning flashes. When the lights return, the COMPANY is strewn about the stage. CREATURE confronts the audience.)

Creature: *(coldly, sings)*
>Now, hear the curse of Frankenstein:
>he was a man who did not
>finish what he had started.
>Frankenstein is cursed!
>Victor Frankenstein!

(VICTOR and ELIZABETH step forward as the CREATURE storms off.)

Elizabeth: *(sings)*
>I've always been there for him
>through the good and the bad.

Victor: *(sings)*
>Elizabeth,
>how can I live without
>you?

39

I am alone without him here.   I can't go on
Why can't I just leave him all alone?   without your
                                                 precious smile.
I need him so.   I need you so.

(HENRY, JUSTINE and ALPHONSE step forward and join VICTOR and ELIZABETH.)

Henry & Justine: *(sing)*
    No one can replace you,   Victor & Elizabeth:
    no one can compare.   Life is empty without you!

Alphonse: *(sings)*
    Victor you're my son.

Henry & Justine: Victor & Elizabeth:
    No one will replace you,   Without you!
    no one will come close!

Alphonse:
    I fear for your life.

E, V, H, J, A: Genevans: *(sing)*
    Others will try   Brightness comes
    to replace your smile,   before the storm,
    that precious smile,   so beware,
    but in the end…   Frankenstein!

Genevans: *(sings)*   Victor: *(sings)*
    Now, hear the tale of   If I were to create a man, yes,
    Frankenstein: if I were to create a man,
    He was a man who   would it not be possible
    sold his soul   to put an end to all death?

Elizabeth, Justine, Alphonse, Henry: *(simultaneously with above)*
    Without you!
    Without you!

Genevans:
    in hopes that he could

accomplish his dream,
COMPANY:
>his dream
>of defeating death.
>Victor Frankenstein!

(CREATURE breaks through the GENEVANS to C., splitting the COMPANY in half.)

Creature: *(sings, pointing at the COMPANY, and audience)*
>You all wanted a monster
>Well, here I am!
>You all made me what I am
>Along with Victor Frankenstein!!!

(There's a bolt of lightning and the lights go dead.)

Blackout.
End of Act I.

Act II
Scene I
Streets of Geneva
Minutes Later

At Rise: *(FRITZ runs into the streets and tries to get people's attention.)*

Fritz: *(sings)*
>Listen up, there's a monster on the loose!

A Woman: *(sings)*
>Be quiet, boy!

Fritz: Listen to me, there's a monster, I say!

Man 1: *(sings)*
>Stop making up this rubbish.

Fritz: Why won't you all just give me a chance
and hear what I have to say?

(A man, ARTHUR, runs in from L.)

Man 2: *(sings)*
>Hey look, it's Arthur Berg!

Man 3: *(sings)*
>He looks like he's seen a ghost!

A Woman: *(sings)*
>Awful dead—

Another Woman: *(sings)*
>—and pale—

All Four:
>—his face is.

Arthur: *(sings)*
>Listen up, there's a killer on the loose!

A Woman: *(sings)*   Fritz: *(sings)*
>A killer, you say?   That's what *I* just said!

Arthur: Listen to me, there's a killer, I say!

Man 4: *(sings)*   Fritz:
     A killer in Geneva?   That's what *I* just said!

Arthur: Why won't you all just listen to me
     and hear what I have to say?

Genevans: *(shouted)*
     Tell us!

(ARTHUR takes a moment to make sure he has everyone's attention, then begins his tale. FRITZ bitterly moves D.L. and separates himself from the nonsense.)

Arthur: *(sings)*
     There I was, just walking through the woods,
     minding my own business,
     when suddenly I came across the hut of old man DeLacey!
     What a sight to see, it was!
     In all my life I have never seen such a horrid sight!

Genevans: *(panicking, sing)*
     There's a killer on the loose!
     There's a killer on the loose!
     Guard your children,
     lock your doors,
     there's a madman on the loose!

     London's had its
     share of killers.
     From Jack the Ripper
     to Sweeney Todd.
     Other towns are
     famous for this
     kind of slaughter fest,
     but not our small town!

     Tell us, tell us more!
     Tell us, tell us now!

Before we go insane!

Arthur: *(breaking up the chaos, sings)*
        Hold ya daisies and ya horses,
        moving right along am I.

(Continuing his tale.)
        Before my startled eyes, stood the hut all burned
        up in Hell's own flames!
        But the worst I am yet to tell!
        You will not believe me when I tell you.
        What a sight to see, it was!
        In all my life I have never seen such a horrid sight!

Genevans: *(panicking again, sing)*
        There's a killer on the loose!
        There's a killer on the loose!
        Stay off the streets,
        stay up late,
        while this killer's on the loose!

        Such a horrid
        murder bloodbath
        has never hit
        our small town!
        Who will he make
        his next victim?
        Will it be me,
        or will it be you?
        What is happening?

        Tell us, tell us more!
        Tell us, tell us now!
        Share all the gossip!

Arthur: *(breaking up the chaos again, sings)*
        Hold ya pansies and ya saddles,
        moving right along am I.

(Continuing his tale.)

Before my startled eyes, there were not one,
but two
of the deadest corpses I have ever seen!
Never have I seen such a bloody massacre.
Poor young William Frankenstein
and old man DeLacey…

Fritz: *(suddenly lashing out, sings)*
What is wrong with you?
What is wrong with you people?
I was just trying to tell you that very news!
I was just trying to say I've seen the killer!

(Seeing that he has finally gotten the crowd's attention, he calms down and continues his story, coloring it up a bit here and there.)
I tell you I saw the best right near DeLacey's hut!
It was a beast at least *(exaggerating)* seven feet tall,
with stitches across his face!

Arthur: *(sings)*
Foolish boy, cut the crap.

Two Women: *(speak, music under)* Don't you know about the boy who cried wolf?

(As the GENEVANS soar into another panic, FRITZ, fed up, exits U.L.)

Genevans: *(sing)*
There's a killer on the loose!
There's a killer on the loose!
Nowhere to run,
you can't hide
while this lunatic's on the loose
in our little town!
In our little town!

(They are distracted by JUSTINE and HENRY running into the streets screaming.)

Justine: Help! Someone please help us!

A Man: *(Moving to comfort her)* Miss Moritz, what's the... *(Noticing WILLIAM'S locket in JUSTINE'S hand)* Where did you get that locket?

Henry: *(confused)* What are you talking about?

A Woman: *(getting a better look)* Doesn't that locket belong to William Frankenstein?

Another Woman: *(peering at the locket)* Yes! That's a picture of Caroline Frankenstein given to William when he was born.

Justine: Well...yes...

Man: *(to ARTHUR, who nods his head in confirmation)* And isn't William Frankenstein dead, now?

Henry: What on Earth are you talking about?

Man: William Frankenstein is found murdered, and Justine Moritz— his trusted nanny—turns up with his locket, a rather valuable trinket, I believe.

Henry: You can't possibly be suggesting that Justine would kill William!

Man: And what motivation would Henry Clerval have for protecting Justine? You wouldn't be trying to protect your fiancé, would you?

Henry: How do *you* know about that?

A Woman: Honestly Henry. The whole town knows about your little secret. You two couldn't keep a secret if your lives depended on it.

Man: And so the conspiracy is revealed.

(By now the GENEVANS have completely surrounded JUSTINE and HENRY, leaving them no escape.)

Interlude

(The lights go dead. An ENSEMBLE creeps into the spotlight looking for any sings of danger.)

Ensemble: *(sings)*
>What has happened to our town called Geneva?
>It was such a peaceful town where we all felt safe.
>What has happened to our town called Geneva?
>We are now so filled with fear of what will happen next!
>
>There is a man named Frankenstein.
>He lives in our town of Geneva.
>Something is wrong with this man.
>Something's very wrong
>With Victor Frankenstein.

(variously)
>Frankenstein was a man who
>sold his soul to the devil.
>Everything that Victor did
>was well meaning,
>but in the end,
>the darkness,
>took control!
>FRANKENSTEIN!!!

(There is a blinding bolt of lightning and the ENSEMBLE disappears.)

Blackout.
End of Scene I.

Act II
Scene II
Frankenstein Chateau Living Room
Two Months Later

At Rise: *(There is a melancholy mood in the air as VICTOR is lying unconscious on the living room couch with ALPHONSE at his aid. VICTOR begins to stir and slowly opens his eyes. Music plays and fades under the scene.)*

Alphonse: Welcome back, son.

Victor: *(groggily)* Father, what happened?

Alphonse: You had a very serious brain fever. You've been unconscious for almost a year.

Victor: A year? *(Dropping his head down on the pillow.)* My God!

Alphonse: *(reluctantly)* But, I'm afraid, that's the good news.

Victor: *(warily)* What's the bad news?

Alphonse: *(hesitating)* I really shouldn't trouble you with this now. You're under enough stress as it is.

Victor: *(pleading)* Father, tell me!

Alphonse: All right. I really think you should wait, but it won't hurt you any less to tell you later. *(Taking in a deep breath, trying to fight off tears.)* Victor, where do I begin? So much has happened while you were sick, so much pain has entered this household.

Victor: Father, please stop torturing me with anticipation! Tell me of the news!

Alphonse: *(sings)*
>You see, it started two weeks ago
>when Henry, Justine and dear William

48

were having a picnic in the woods.
Dear William wondered off all alone
and never ever came back alive.
He was murdered in the woods that day!

Victor: *(music under)* Murdered? How can that be? What monster would murder such an innocent child as my dearest brother, William? Tell me, father, now! Please tell me that they've found the heartless murderer of my dearest brother, William!

Alphonse: *(sings)*
Victor, I don't know how to say this.
I still have not come to terms with the truth.
Justine has been charged and convicted
for the death of our dearest William!
Justine shall hang in the morning!

Victor: *(music under)* Justine? How can that be? Why would Justine murder William? She loved him with all her heart! Please tell me father, that Justine is not the murderer of my dearest brother, William!

Alphonse: *(turning away, music under)* Victor, I'm so sorry. I should not have told you so soon after you woke up.

Victor: Father, please stop torturing me like this! What evidence could they possibly have against Justine?

Alphonse: *(sings)*
You see, when they found our dear William,
the locket of your dearest mother,
was not found around our dear William's neck!
Instead it was found in Justine's hands!
The locket was worth a good fortune.
They say she killed him for the locket!
(music ends)

Victor: *(stunned)* This can't be! I have to see her!

Alphonse: *(trying to keep VICTOR in bed)* Henry is with her now. Poor thing is heart-broken. Their secret engagement was exposed by the whole thing. Henry tried to protect her, but the courts would not listen, seeing as he was engaged to her. Oh dear, I knew I shouldn't have told you about it so soon. Look at you, you're a nervous wreck.

Victor: Father, you don't understand, I *have* to see Justine!

Alphonse: *(resting a hand on VICTOR'S shoulder)* There's nothing you can do for her—

Victor: For Christ's sake, Father, let me go!

(VICTOR breaks away from ALPHONSE and exits U.C. Music plays under scene change.)

Blackout.
End of Scene II.

Act II
Scene III
Justine's Jail Cell
Minutes Later

Setting: Typical jail cell—empty except for a washing basin and a bed.

At Rise: *(JUSTINE and HENRY are embracing each other, tear stricken.)*

Both: *(sing)*
>No one can replace you,
>no one can compare.
>No one will replace you,
>no one will come close.

Henry: *(rising)*
>How can I go on without your smile,
>that precious smile, to comfort me?
(HENRY lowers back down to his knees.)
Both: No one can replace you
>no one can compare.

(They fall into each other's arms and begin crying. VICTOR is led into the cell by a GUARD and left alone with HENRY and JUSTINE. At VICTOR'S entrance, JUSTINE throws herself at VICTOR'S feet, crying.)

Justine: Victor, can you ever forgive me?

Victor: *(kneeling down, eye-to-eye)* Just tell me that you didn't do what you say you did.

Justine: *(unable to make eye contact)* Of course I didn't! Did I have any choice? I knew that I'd never be able to prove my innocence and I hoped that they might show a little mercy if I pleaded guilty. It was wrong, I know, but I didn't know what else to do!

51

Victor: *(uneasily)* Justine, you were there when William was murdered, weren't you?

Justine: *(unable to meet his eyes)* Yes...

Victor: You saw the killer, didn't you?

Justine: *(shaking)* Yes, I did.

Henry: We saw no such thing. It was nothing more than a waking nightmare. That's all.

Justine: How can you say that? You were *there*! You saw that...thing!

Henry: It was nothing more than a nightmare. That's all.

Victor: *(ignoring HENRY, looks her straight in the eye)* Justine, tell me who it was.

(JUSTINE hesitates, then rises, pleading with VICTOR.)

Justine: I can't tell you. Please don't make me tell you what I saw.

Henry: You saw nothing!

Victor: Justine, for William's sake, tell me!

(JUSTINE hesitates then slowly rises, not making eye contact.)

Justine: *(sings)*
>Victor, I trust you with this deep secret
>that I alone can tell about his death.
>We were there on that day of William's death.
>I swear to you, the Devil killed your brother.
>
>I know it must be hard to believe me
>but I know what I saw; it was Satan.
>He was a hideous beast from Hell!
>I swear to you, the Devil killed your brother.

52

(speaks, music under) He was at least six feet tall, and covered with hideous stitches. His skin was drawn tightly over his bones as if he were sewn together. Oh, you must think me mad!

(VICTOR has turned completely pale, realizing just exactly who it was that killed WILLIAM.)

Justine: *(sings)*
> Victor, you're turning pale! I'm so sorry.
> I have no intentions of grieving you!
> I know it must be hard to believe me
> but I swear to you, the Devil killed your brother.

Victor: *(sings)*
> Justine, I believe you, for I have seen
> this beast you speak of, this beast from Hell.
> I blame myself
> for William's death.
> I promise you I am
> at fault for William's death.

Henry: *(sings, simultaneously with above)*
> Justine, don't talk nonsense
> we saw no beast!
> I promise you
> the Devil did not kill William!

Justine & Victor: *(yelling at HENRY)* We know he did!

(HENRY stares at them, stunned, and VICTOR turns to JUSTINE.)

Victor: Justine, I promise you, whether you see another sunrise after tomorrow or not, I will avenge the death of my brother and put your name to justice.

Justine: Thank you.

(HENRY lets out a sigh as the lights fade out.)

Interlude

(JUSTINE slowly and remorsefully enters a spotlight.)

Justine: *(sings)*
> In memoria aeterna.
> Rit justus domine.
>
> Why, my Lord, why must it end?
> Why do you have to put us through such pain?
> Why must we feel the pain of losing our loved ones?
> Why, my Lord, must it end?
> Why can't it just go on and on?
> > **Blackout.**
> > **End of Scene III.**

Act II
Scene IV
The Geneva Gallows
The Next Morning

At Rise: *(JUSTINE is led onto the gallows at C. by the EXECUTIONER.[2] The FRANKENSTEINS, comforting HENRY who is near tears, stand off to the side. The GENEVANS begin to chant "Hang Her!")*

Executioner: *(music under)* Do you have any last words?

Justine: *(sings)*
> I only want to say a few short words.
> I don't want this day to be remembered as
> the day that William's death was avenged,
> but as the day that Justine Moritz was killed, too.

(The GENEVANS, becoming discontent, start to chant "Kill her!")

Justine:
> I'm trusting my soul in my
> Lord's own hands.
> I pray for this killer
> to be punished.
> And as you lay me down,
> remember this:
> This was the day
> that Justine Moritz was killed, too.

Henry: *(sings)*
> No one can replace you,
> no one can compare.
> No one will replace you,
> no one will come close.
> How can I go on
> without your smile—
> that precious smile—
> To comfort me?

(Through this, the GENEVANS begin chanting "Hang her!" again and the EXECUTIONER slides the noose over JUSTINE'S head. JUSTINE backs up over the trap door, and the EXECUTIONER releases the trap. HENRY, falling to his knees, lets out a blood-curdling scream as lightning strikes.)

---

[2] It is recommended that the part of the EXECUTIONER be played by the CREATURE.

Henry: WHY MY LORD!?

Interlude

(The lights go out, leaving VICTOR in the spotlight.)

Victor: *(sings)*
>There is a man named Frankenstein;
>He lives in this town of Geneva…

(The lights come up on the graveyard, and VICTOR crosses to his mother's grave.)

Segue From Scene IV Into:

Act II
Scene V
Genevan Graveyard
Early Morning: Later That Week

At Rise: *(The Geneva bells ring throughout the night and strike three.)*

Victor: *(near tears, sings)*
>There's a hole in my soul where you used to be.
>I've tried to forget the pain,
>but it keeps coming back to me.
>I can never let go.
>
>Everything I've done, I've done it for you,
>hoping to bring you back into my life.
>Why can't I put you behind me?
>I can never go.

(ELIZABETH enters from L., then stops when she sees VICTOR and decides to wait before approaching him.)

Victor: *(sings)*
>I blame myself for what has happened.
>I only wanted to bring you back!

Why can't I let go?

I must move on, I have to let go.
But I will never for get the memory!
I love you so, my dear mother,
but I have to let go!
I must let go.

(VICTOR breaks down, crying. ELIZABETH crosses over to comfort him. He jumps up, startled by her presence and quickly wipes the tears from his eyes.)

Victor: Elizabeth, I'm sorry. You just startled me.

Elizabeth: *(placing a hand on his cheek)* Victor, you have to stop blaming yourself for the deaths of everyone who's close to you. Death is something that none of us can do anything about, we just have to accept it.

Victor: *(coldly)* You're wrong, Elizabeth. Unfortunately, there is something that we can do about death.

Elizabeth: Victor, will you stop talking this nonsense? William and Justine are dead! It's not your fault!

Victor: *(rising)* Elizabeth, I'm so sorry for causing you so much pain. I never meant to bring harm to any of you.

Elizabeth: Victor, *you* haven't brought harm to anyone. You have got to stop talking like this! I know you've been going through a hard time, we all have. It doesn't mean that you have to alienate yourself from the rest of your family. *We're* still alive, Victor. The time has to come when you stop focusing on the ones who are gone and start focusing on the ones who are still here.

Victor: Elizabeth, you're right.

(VICTOR reaches into his pocket, pulls out the engagement ring, and gets down on one knee.)

Victor: *(sings)*
>From that moment when I first saw your face,
>I knew that you would always be mine!
>I knew that we would never part
>as long as we are both alive.

(ELIZABETH takes the ring and places it on her finger, near tears, as VICTOR rises and takes her hands in his.)
>For so long, I've run away from life.
>I'd left my dreams and fears far behind me.
>I could not bear to face the world
>my life had become.
>But you are my light,
>my sun, my moon,
>my only blessed star.
>My life is empty without you.

Together:
>Without you!

>From this day on, I vow that I will live
>for no one but you, my dear!
>I've waited so long
>for when you (we) will be mine (one)!
>My life is worth nothing
>if I cannot share it with you.
>My life is empty without you.
>My life is empty without you.

(They kiss and start to exit L., hand in hand. Suddenly, recorder music rings throughout the graveyard and VICTOR freezes.)

Victor: Elizabeth, why don't you go on ahead, I just want to say good-bye to mother.

Elizabeth: *(smiling)* Don't take long.

(They kiss lightly on the lips and ELIZABETH exits L. VICTOR turns around and looks around the graveyard.)

Victor: *(calling out)* Who's there? Hello?

58

(At that, CREATURE rises from behind the C. gravestone, stunning VICTOR who hasn't seen CREATURE since its "birth.")

Victor: *(sings)*
>Fiend!
>Get out of my sight,
>you horrid wretch!
>What the Hell was I thinking
>creating such a monster?
>
>Beast!
>What was I thinking?
>You're a horrid wretch!
>Get out of my sight you fiend
>and bother me no—

(CREATURE, unhurt by VICTOR'S harsh words, chuckles and approaches VICTOR, who backs away. As the CREATURE cuts in, VICTOR stares in disbelief, not able to accept that CREATURE can talk.)

Creature: *(cutting in, sings)*
>Foolish Frankenstein, do you really think
>that your harsh words can sting my cold soul now?
>After all this time I have but one thing to ask of you,
>dear Victor Frankenstein.

Victor: *(music under)* Never! I will never become the slave of such a loathsome murderer!

(CREATURE turns on VICTOR, startling him.)

Creature: *(sings)*
>Cursed Frankenstein I only ask
>that you lend me your ear and hear
>what it is that I have to ask of you.
>I will not soon forget that cursed night
>when you left me for dead.

(speaks, music under) You cannot understand the pain that I have undergone. I have been completely rejected by your fellow men.

Victor: *(music under)* You killed my brother, why?

Creature: *(music under)* I killed your brother to bring into your life the same pain that you brought into mine.

Victor: And Justine? What did she do to deserve the fate that belonged to you?

Creature: *(sings)*
> For most of my life, I've lived alone.
> Darkness has become part of my life.
> All that I want is some companionship,
> someone to show me how to live,
> how to see the light.
>
> Someone like me is all I want from life.
> Someone who can relate to the pain I have felt.
> Someone who will show me how to live and to love.
> Just one person like me.

(speaks, music under) I want a mate, a female. Someone who will share my pain, and my love. This, at least, you owe me, Frankenstein.

Victor: *(quietly, music under)* Never.

Creature: What makes you, Victor Frankenstein, worthy of being loved? What made that girl worthy of being loved by your dear friend Henry? What makes me, your creation, unworthy of being loved? What have all of you that I have not?

(VICTOR remains silent, undecided.)

Creature: *(sings)*
> You brought me into this world of hate.
> This world has become all of my sadness.
> Do you not feel that you owe me this?
> I have never known the true love I long to know.
>
> Someone like me is all I want from life.
> Someone who can relate to the pain I have felt.

60

Someone who will show me how to live and to love.
Just one person like me.

Someone like me is all I want from life.
Someone who can relate to the pain I have felt.
Someone who will show me how to live and to love.
Just one person, just one person, just one person,
just one person like me.

(music ends, speaks) If you grant me this simple wish, I promise that my mate and I will disappear from the eyes of man. Don't you feel that you owe me this much after all of the pain that you have caused me?

(VICTOR, conscience-stricken, crosses C., struggling with his decision.)

Victor: *(to himself, music under)* If I say yes, what would be the worst that could happen? He and his mate will disappear and never be seen again. *(To CREATURE)* And if I say no?

Creature: *(under his voice, sings)*
I'll be with you on your wedding night,
I promise you, Victor Frankenstein.

(VICTOR slowly crosses to C.)
Victor: *(sings)*
Oh Lord, please tell me now, what should I do?
Satisfy this beast or live a life of fear?
Why must *I* choose? Why *me*?
Why Frankenstein?
Did I ask for this life of pain?…
(speaks, to CREATURE) I suppose that I owe you this wish, as long as you promise to leave and never bother mankind or myself again.

Creature: This I do.

Both: *(shaking hands)* Then we have a deal.

Blackout.
End of Act II.
61

Act III
Scene I
Frankenstein Chateau
Later That Week

At Rise: *(ALPHONSE, HENRY and ELIZABETH enter through the U.C. door.)*

Elizabeth: Henry, he's returned to his lab. We have to do something before we lose him again!

Alphonse: *(pleading)* Yes, Henry, please help us!

Henry: *(looking up to the attic)* Don't worry, I'll put a stop to this nonsense once and for all.

(HENRY crosses to the stairwell door and knocks loudly.)

Henry: Victor! Come down, right now! We need to talk. Victor, I know you can hear me, so come down right now!

(For a moment, there is silence. Then, VICTOR'S reluctant steps can be heard descending the stair case. As ALPHONSE, ELIZABETH, and HENRY wait impatiently, VICTOR enters through the door.)

Victor: *(impatiently, music under)* What do you want, Henry?

Henry: *(music under)* We need to talk, Victor.

Victor: *(beginning to leave, music under)* I don't have time for this.

Alphonse: *(strictly, sings)*
  Victor listen up,
  we are very concerned
  about your health.
  You lock yourself
  inside your lab
  all day and night.

Victor: *(sings)*

We're so concerned	Father,
about your health,	please don't
we never ever see you now.	worry about me.
Please tell us	No matter
about this darkness	what,
that has plagued your soul	I will not succumb
for so long.	to this darkness.

(to ELIZABETH)

Victor, this is wrong	Dearest, fear not
you should not have	no harm will
to throw your life away.	find us.
Victor, please fear not.	Elizabeth,
We only want to help you.	I love you so
through this hard time.	much.

Elizabeth: *(simultaneously with above, sings)*

Victor there is
something wrong
with you right now.
What has happened to you?
You have been possessed
for so long.

Alphonse: Victor: *(to HENRY)*

Victor, you're my son,	Henry, fear not,
I'm scared to say	I'm in
I fear for your life.	control.
Victor I am scared.	I failed last time
I love you so.	I will not
I do not want to lose you.	again.

Elizabeth: *(simultaneously with above)*   Henry:

Victor	Victor what's this curse
please tell	that has plagued your
	soul?
me about	I feel that you know not
your work.	what you're going
	through.

Dearest,
I'm scared
that I'll
lose you.
Please don't leave me.

There was once a spark
in your shining eyes.
But, now I only see
a dead lake of darkness.

(An ENSEMBLE appears at either side of the chateau.)

Alphonse:

Victor, listen up,
We are very concerned
about your health.
Please tell us
about this darkness
that has plagued your soul
for so long.

Victor: *(to ALPHONSE)*

Father, please don't
worry about me.
(to ELIZABETH)
Eliz-
-abeth,
I love you so
much.

Elizabeth: *(simultaneously with above)*

Victor
there is

something wrong
with you right now.

Dearest,
I'm scared
that I'll lose you.
Please don't leave me.

Henry:

Victor what's this curse
that has plagued your
soul?
I feel that you know not
what you're going
through.
There once was a spark
in your shining eyes.
But, now I only see
a dead lake of darkness.

Ensemble: *(simultaneously with above, sings)*

There is a man named Frankenstein.
He lives in our town of Geneva.
Something is wrong with this man
named Frankenstein,
Victor Frankenstein!

(VICTOR breaks down and screams out at the top of his lungs. ENSEMBLE disappears.)

Victor: For Christ's sake, let me be!

64

Interlude

(As the lights go dead, the others back off, leaving VICTOR on his knees in the spotlight.)

Victor: *(sings)*
> If I were to create a man,
> yes, if I were to create a man,
> would it not be possible
> to put an end to all death?
> Families would suffer no more;
> Lovers would never separate;
> And no one would ever again feel
> the pain that has become my life…
>
> What has happened?
> What has gone wrong?
> All I wished was to serve man.
> But not at the expense of my loved ones!
> How, God, can you ask me
> to make such a sacrifice?
>
> What has happened?
> What has gone wrong?
> I used to be so alive.
> But now my soul is dead.
> Why, my Lord,
> why must I be
> put through so much suffering?
>
> I once knew light,
> but now, only empty darkness.
> Lord, please show me the way
> back into the light!
> If only I could be given the chance,
> I'd take it all back,
> just to have things the way they were.
> Lord, please lead me back into the light!

Blackout.
End of Scene I.

65

Act III
Scene II
Victor's Lab
Later That Week

At Rise: *(A bolt of lightning lights up the scene. VICTOR has returned to his lab and is not-so-eagerly performing the experiments of his past.)*

Victor: *(sadly, sings)*
>All these tests,
>all these memories,
>coming back at once to me.
>I can feel the darkness
>coming back to me.
>All my fears, all my nightmares
>suddenly coming true.

(panicking)
>But what if my monster's mate
>is just as evil as her spouse?
>I will have let another monster free!

(scolding himself)
>Stop it!

>He will come and like my life away
>if I do not obey his wishes!

(A bolt of lightning and VICTOR turns to the equipment and begins hesitantly putting it together.)

Victor:
>All these machines,
>all of my fears.
>What is wrong with me?
>I can feel my nightmares
>around the bend.

All my fears, all my nightmares
suddenly coming true.

(panicking)
        But what if this new monster
        does not agree to disappear from man?
        Or what if they breed and create
        a new mankind?
(scolding himself, again)
        Stop it!

(HENRY approaches the D.R. door from the "stair case" and begins pounding on the door.)

Henry: *(sings)*
        Victor you've disappeared into your again!
        We have to put an end to this nonsense!

(A bolt of lightning and TWO GENEVANS appear at either side of the chateau and start chanting "Frankenstein, Frankenstein, Victor Frankenstein!" VICTOR begins to raise the operating table toward the ceiling.)

Henry: *(pounding on the door, sings)*
        Victor, open up!

Victor: *(sings)*
        Look at this,
        it's almost done.
        I can't believe my eyes.
        My nightmare's coming true again
        right before my eyes.
        All my fears, all my nightmares,
        suddenly coming true.

Henry: *(simultaneously with above)*
        Victor why won't you let me in?
        Victor open up this door I say!
        Victor this is insane!
        Let me in!

Why won't you let me help you?
Victor, open up!

Vic. & Ens.: *(sing)*   Henry:
  All my/his fears!   Open this door!
  All my/his nightmares!   Listen to me
                             Frankenstein!
Victor:
  Suddenly coming true!   Enough of all of this!

(HENRY loses his patience, kicks down the door and bursts into the lab. The ENSEMBLE disappears.)

Henry: *(indicating the equipment, music under)* What is all of this, Victor?

Victor: *(irritated, music under)* Stay out of my affairs, Henry.

Henry: *(shocked)* "Stay out of *your* affairs?" Victor, Justine is dead. We were engaged to be married. I believe that your work has something to do with her death, so you had better damn believe that this is my business.

Victor: *(losing his patience)* Henry, I *do* blame myself for Justine's death.

Henry: You blame yourself? Well, I'm very glad to hear that, Victor Frankenstein.

Victor: Henry, let me be.

Henry: No. For once in my life, I'm not going to let you be. And I'm putting an end to this nightmare—*(HENRY grabs a large piece of wood and begins beating the equipment)*—once and for all!

(VICTOR stares in disbelief as he watches the sparks fly. His attitude quickly changes and he begins to beg HENRY to stop.)

Victor: Please Henry, stop this! You don't know what you're doing!

Henry: Oh, yes I do. This is for William *(swings at a machine)*, this is for Justine *(swings at another machine)*, and this is for your fam—

(As HENRY swings his stick at the next machine, CREATURE emerges from behind it, grabs the stick from HENRY'S grasp with one hand and clutches HENRY'S throat with the other hand. Lightning strikes. As HENRY chokes to death, VICTOR, enraged, charges at CREATURE who easily pushes VICTOR away with his free hand. As HENRY'S body goes limp, the CREATURE tosses the dead body to the floor and VICTOR starts cursing at CREATURE.)

Victor: *(sings)*
    Beast!
    Get out of my life
    your murderer!
    What the Hell was I thinking
    creating another beast?

    Fiend!
    What was I thinking?
    Leave me alone, fiend!
    Get out of my life, you fiend!
    And bother me no more!

(At that, VICTOR cuts the rope holding the operating table up in the air. CREATURE watches in horror as the operating table comes crashing to the floor. Body parts fly off the operating table as it crashes. CREATURE rushes to VICTOR and grabs him around the throat.)

Creature: *(sings)*
    Listen to me now, Frankenstein!
    I will not forgive me, I'll not forget
    what you have done to me this night.
    You call me a monster, you wretched man
    But it's *you* who's made me so.
    Remember that on your wedding night,
    Victor Frankenstein!

(At that, the CREATURE lunges out the window into the rain. ELIZABETH rushes up the "stair well" and bursts into the lab to see what the commotion was about.)

Elizabeth: Victor! What happened?

Victor: Henry burst in and started beating up all the equipment and…there was an explosion and—

(He shakily points a finger at HENRY's body. ELIZABETH gasps and looks away from the corpse. Then, fighting off tears, crosses to VICTOR and embraces him.)

Elizabeth: Victor, if you want to postpone the wedding, I'll understand.

Victor: *(wiping away his tears, sings)*
    Elizabeth, please don't worry.
    A terrible darkness
    has fallen on us.
    But we must not succumb.
    We shall lift lamps
    and find our way through the night.

    From that moment when
    I first saw your face
    I knew that you would always be mine!
    I knew that we would
    never part as long as
    we are both still alive.
(speaks) Elizabeth, I wouldn't postpone our wedding for the world. Now, I am finally ready to put this nightmare behind me. It's time to move on and stop dwelling on the past.

Creature Voice: *(sings)*
    I'll be with you on your wedding night
    I promise you, Victor Frankenstein.
(VICTOR shudders and embraces ELIZABETH, who did not hear the voice.)

Blackout.
End of Scene II.

Act III
Scene III
Geneva Park
One Month Later

Setting: Wedding reception for Victor and Elizabeth. Basically same set as Streets of Geneva only with dinner tables set up on either side of the stage.

At Rise: *(The* Wedding March *can be heard being played on an organ and the door of the church swings open as VICTOR and ELIZABETH exit, followed by the GENEVANS and ALPHONSE. A WEDDING BAND*, consisting of two FIDDLES, two RECORDERS [one of which is played by the CREATURE], a DOUBLE BASS, and a TAMBOURINE/BONGO DRUM PLAYER, sets up at R. The BAND MEMBERS, including the CREATURE, are all wearing hooded robes. ALPHONSE crosses U.C. and begins clinking his wine glass to make a speech.)*

Alphonse: *(sings)*
> I remember the day that we
> brought this young little girl to our home.
> An orphan at the age of six,
> she was the saddest child in the world.
> *(to ELIZABETH)*
> We always knew that you and VICTOR
> would one day be united.
> And now that day is here—

Victor: *(to ELIZABETH)*
> —Now that you are mine.

Elizabeth:
> —Now that we are one.

Alphonse:
> On this joyous day!

---

* The orchestra is cued to replace the Wedding Band should the actors cast in the roles not be able to perform.

(The BAND strikes up on an upbeat dance and VICTOR and ELIZABETH start dancing as the crowd claps/stomps along with the beat.)

COMPANY: *(sings)*
On this joyous day of high spirits
two souls are merged into one.
May joy and love spread to all
on this joyous day of love.

(During the following, VICTOR notices that the tallest BAND MEMBER [the CREATURE] every once in a while breaks off from the music and plays the CREATURE'S "recorder theme." VICTOR recognizes the music, but tries to hide his alarm. ELIZABETH notices his concern but doesn't say anything. VICTOR and ELIZABETH both keep their eyes on the hooded figure. The WOMEN start to dance while the MEN chant "Joyous, joyous day!" Then they trade off, the MEN showing off for the WOMEN while the WOMEN chant "On this joyous! On this joyous!")

COMPANY:
On this joyous day!

(The COMPANY joins together for the finale of the song, performing an elaborate dance. ALPHONSE and CREATURE, who puts his recorder off to the side, join in the dance. Throughout the dance, ALPHONSE gets more and more tired, clutching to his chest, but he continues on. As everybody trades off their partner, VICTOR and ELIZABETH get farther apart from each other—and ELIZABETH gets closer to CREATURE. Throughout this dance, VICTOR and ELIZABETH, growing more panicked, keep trying to get back together, but only get farther apart.)

COMPANY:
On this joyous day of high spirits
two souls are merged into one.
May joy and love spread to all
on this joyous—
on this joyous—
on this joyous—

72

(Now, at the apex of the song, VICTOR is at L. and ELIZABETH is partnered up with the hooded CREATURE at R.)

Victor and Elizabeth: *(calling out to each other)*
       On this joyous—
COMPANY:
       On this joyous—

(CREATURE throws back his hood and grabs ELIZABETH around the throat. ALPHONSE, his heart weak from dancing, clutches his chest and falls to the ground in a seizure. The crowd goes mad. The WOMEN scream and flee, some of the MEN comfort their wives, some try to attack CREATURE who easily blocks their attacks with one hand while holding the choking ELIZABETH with the other. Through all of this, VICTOR tries to get through the mob to the CREATURE, but it's too chaotic for him to get through. As ELIZABETH dies in the CREATURE'S arms, CREATURE yells out to VICTOR above the roar of the mob.)

Creature: *(music under)* I warned you, Frankenstein! You denied me my bride, and so I deny you yours!

(CREATURE drops ELIZABETH'S limp body to the ground and picks up the dinner table nearest him and uses it to push back the angry MOB while he makes his escape U.R. behind the church. The lights go out on stage and the MOB moves into the aisles of the audience.)

Segue From Scene III Into:

Act III
Scene IV
Streets of Geneva
Moments Later

At Rise: *(The MOB is quickly growing Hell-bent on finding the CREATURE as they march through the aisles trying to find him.)*

Mob: *(sings)*
       We must find this monster!

73

We must catch this beast from Hell!
(variously)
 We must find this monster!
 We must catch this beast from Hell!

(As the MOB begins to chant "Find it! Kill it! Slay the Beast!" A MOBSTER steps up into a spotlight and begins prepping up the MOB.)

Mobster 1: *(sings)*
 Listen up we must find
 this beast from Hell!
 We must destroy this creature—
 this beast from Hell!

Mob: Too many have died in this small town
 at the hands of this creature—
 this beast from Hell!

 We must kill this creature!
 We must slay this horrid wretch!
(variously)
 We must kill this creature!
 We must slay this horrid wretch!

(As the MOB begins to chant "Hunt it! Burn it! Kill the best!" another MOBSTER steps up and begins prepping the MOB.)

Mobster 2:
 Listen up we must kill
 this horrid wretch!
 We have to put an end
 to its carnage!

Mob: Too many have died in this small town
 at the hands of this creature—
 this beast from Hell!

 We must slay this cruel fiend!
 We must not let it escape!
(variously)

74

We must slay this cruel fiend!
We must not let it escape!

(As the MOB begins to chant "Hunt it! Track it! Find the beast!" a third MOBSTER steps up in front and begins to prep the MOB while FRITZ tries to get the grown-ups' attention.)

Mobster 3:	Fritz: *(sings)*
We must claim revenge on	Listen up, I have seen
this murderer.	this beast from Hell!
Justine and William's blood	Why won't you listen up?
is on his hands!	I have seen it!

Mob: Too many have died in this small town
at the hands of this creature—
this beast from Hell!

(They wander off chanting "Revenge for William! Revenge for Justine! Revenge for Henry! Revenge for the Frankensteins!")

Blackout.
End of Scene IV.

Act III
Scene V
Geneva Park
Moments Later

At Rise: *(The park is completely dark except for an eerie light cast across VICTOR who is cradling ELIZABETH'S dead body in his arms D.R. In the background, we can hear the MOB's chanting fading into the distance.)*

Victor: *(sings)*
> Where have they gone,
> the old familiar faces?
> Once, I had a monther,
> but she died and left me.
> She died prematurely
> on a day of horrors.
> All are gone,
> the old familiar faces.
>
> Where have they gone,
> the old familiar faces?
> Once, I had a brother,
> but he died, and left me.
> An angel of angels
> taken from this world.
> All are gone,
> the old familiar faces.
>
> Where have they gone,
> the old familiar faces?
> Once, I had a playmate.
> Once, I had a best friend
> in my days of childhood,
> in my joyful school days.
> All are gone,
> the old familiar faces.
>
> Where have they gone,

the old familiar faces?
Once, I had a love,
fairest of all the stars:
Her doors are now closed on me,
she is now long gone.
All are gone,
the old familiar faces.

Where have they gone,
the old familiar faces?
Once I had a family,
but now, they all are gone.
They wall were taken from me;
All are departed.
All are gone,
the old familiar faces.

(FRITZ enters the scene from L. with a pistol and a torch. When VICTOR sees him enter, he rises and screams at the boy.)

Victor: Leave me alone! Leave me alone to die here in my self-hatred!

(FRITZ, more confused than scared, begins to run away.)

Victor: Wait! Wait. Why is such a young man like yourself involved in such a violent riot?

Fritz: *(eyeing VICTOR with extreme paranoia)* Well, see you sir, I ran into the monster several months ago, sir. But no one believed me when I told them, sir, and now they all know that I was telling the truth, sir. So I want to help, sir, to find the monster, sir.

Victor: *(looking at ELIZABETH)* How far are you willing to go to see the end of this... "monster."

Fritz: Far as I need to, sir.

Victor: That's your dream, isn't it? To see justice done? To see things right in the world? And you're willing to give up everything you have left to see it through, aren't you? Trust me, I've been there. The reality isn't anywhere near as beautiful as the dream.

(FRIZT stares blankly at VICTOR for a few moments, speechless, then VICTOR signals for him to leave. FRITZ quickly begins to leave.)

Victor: Wait, come back. *(FRITZ impatiently comes back)* Leave me your gun.

Fritz: But sir, if I leave you with my gun, sir, what will I have to defend myself against the beast, sir?

Victor: *(chuckling to himself)* Defend yourself against the beast? Silly boy, you won't need to defend yourself against the beast as long as you stay as far away from where I am as possible. The…"beast" will be here soon enough…if he isn't here already.

(FRITZ lowers the gun to the floor and runs out of the park before VICTOR can call him back again. VICTOR rises and slowly walks to the gun, picks it up and crosses to ELIZABETH.)

Victor: *(calling into the darkness)* Where are you? I know you're out there! How dare you not face me!!!! You wanted to make my soul as wretched as your form, well you've succeeded. Now come out and face me like the beast that you are.

Creature: *(emerging from the darkness)* I have no fight with you.

Victor: You have no fight with me? You take my life away, you ruin the very being of my soul, and yet you claim to have no fight with me?

Creature: I want nothing more of you, Frankenstein. I do not wish to take your life, for to do so would be an unjust mercy on your soul. You could have killed me that night when you made me, but you didn't. You let me loose into the wild to suffer the cruelties of this world without the guidance and love of a parent. I could kill you now, but I won't.

Victor: If you will not fight me, then I will fight you! *(He shoots CREATURE in the arm. CREATURE collapses to the ground in pain,*

78

clutching his wounded arm. VICTOR sings, circling around the CREATURE)

>Here, tonight, I end it now;
>This waking nightmare that has haunted me!
>No more shall die at your hands!
>Now I will end this nightmare!

(As VICTOR begins to pull the trigger, CREATURE knocks the gun from his hand and begins to wrestle with VICTOR. FRITZ runs on, leading the MOB behind him. He sees his gun on the ground and goes for it. He aims and fires at CREATURE, but misses and hits VICTOR instead.)

Creature: *(screaming in agony)* Father!!!!

Victor: *(as he fades out)* Elizabeth…

(The GENEVANS charge at the CREATURE who retreats into the church, apparently barring the door behind him so that they can't get in. Soon after he appears on the roof of the church. As FRITZ aims and prepares to shoot, the CREATURE yells out.)

Creature: Listen to me Geneva!!!
(seeing that he has the GENEVANS' attention, he sings)

>You hate me, yet you've never met me.
>You judge me, yet you do not know me.
>How can you justify killing me now?
>How can you excuse the way I've been treated?
>
>Someone like me, was all I wanted from life
>Someone who could relate to the pain I have felt
>Someone who would show me how to live and to love
>Just one person like me.
>
>Am I a beast or a man?
>I was brought into this world
>by a man who did not want me.
>I was shunned from this world
>by the people of this town.
>So I ask you here, tonight,

am *I* the beast,
or is it all of *you*?

A monster like me, is what you all created
You could have shown me love, but all you gave was hate
So now I shall leave you and this wretched life
No more shall the hideous creation
of Victor Frankenstein
plague this world of yours!

(He raises his arms to the sky and is struck by a bolt of lightning as the lights blackout.)

Blackout.
End of Act III.

Epilogue
Geneva Graveyard
Midnight-Years Later

Setting: The center tombstone is marked "Victor Frankenstein," the operating table is high above the stage, and there are candles placed all over the graveyard.

Interlude

(Darkness. A PRIEST appears in a small spotlight.)

Priest: *(music under)* It has been ten years since Victor Frankenstein and his Holy abomination were killed. On this night—the anniversary of their deaths—we, the people of Geneva, gather here in the cemetery and remember – we remember the tale of Victor Frankenstein.

At Rise: *(Lightning. The COMPANY surrounds the C. grave in a semi-circle. ALPHONSE, JUSTINE, HENRY, and ELIZABETH are standing in front of the group. The four are wearing dirty, torn clothes, as if they've been buried and come back from the dead. They all have pale complexions. HENRY and ELIZABETH have bruises around their necks from the CREATURE'S choking hands. JUSTINE has a bruise around her neck from the noose.)*

Henry: *(sings)*   Justine: *(sings)*
    There was a man named   Justine: *(sings)*
    Frankenstein;   Victor Frankenstein!
Elizabeth: *(sings)*
    He lived in this town   Alphonse: *(sings)*
    of Geneva.   Victor Frankenstein!

All Four: *(variously)*
    Something was wrong with this man.
    Something was very wrong
    With Victor Frankenstein!

(A bolt of lightning strikes and when the lights return, DELACEY has taken the stage and is also wearing dirty, tattered – and singed –

clothing. ALPHONSE, HENRY, JUSTINE and ELIZABETH have moved into the semi-circle.)

DeLacey: *(sings)*
    Now, hear the tale of Frankenstein:
    He was a man who
    Sold his soul
    in hopes that he could
    accomplish his dream,
    his dream of defeating Death.
    Victor Frankenstein!

Henry:
    Victor Frankenstein!
Justine:
    Victor Frankenstein!

Alphonse & Elizabeth:
    Victor Frankenstein!

(A bolt of lightning and when the lights return, WILLIAM and FRITZ have taken the stage and DELACEY has joined the semi-circle. WILLIAM, also, is dressed in dirty, tattered clothing has a pale complexion and has the bruises around his neck from the CREATURE'S mark.)

Fritz and William: *(sings)*
    Pie Jesu domine dona eis requiem.
    Lord, bring back dear Frankenstein!

(WILLIAM and FRITZ step back and join the semi-circle.)

COMPANY: *(sings)*
    All he wanted was to end death!
    But instead he brought on the deaths
    of those who were closest of all to him!
    Where is Frankenstein,
    Victor Frankenstein?

(The BASES begin chanting "Frankenstein, Frankenstein, where is Frankenstein?" as they circle around the group, and walk into the aisles of the audience, searching for VICTOR. The VICTIMS chant "Frankenstein, Victor Frankenstein" variously.)

Genevans: *(variously)*
    Agnus dei qui tollis
    peccata mundi!
    Dona eis requiem!

Frankenstein!
Frankenstein!
Frankenstein!
Frankenstein!
FRANKENSTEIN!!!

(Throughout the chant, the operating table has been lowering and we see a body covered by a white sheet. At the end of the chant, VICTOR, who had been on the operating table, sits straight up and tosses the white sheet aside as the CREATURE rises up from the C. grave. A bolt of lightning and when the lights return, the FULL COMPANY is on stage, with VICTOR and the CREATURE U.C.)

Victor: *(sings)*
    Now hear the tale of Frankenstein:
    Victor Frankenstein!

Creature: *(sings)*
Victor Frankenstein!
He was a man who sold his soul
in hopes that he could—

    —accomplish—
Both: —his dream—
Victor: —of defeating death.
Creature:
    Victor Frankenstein!

GENEVANS: *(sing)*
    Victor Frankenstein!

Creature & Victims:
    Now, hear the tale of Frankenstein:

GENEVANS:
Franknestein!/Victor Frankenstein!

Victor & Victims:
    He lost everything that he had—

Frankenstein!/Victor Frankenstein!

COMPANY:
    —because he meddled in God's affairs.
    That's all—
Men: —there is to this story.
Women:
    —of Victor Frankenstein!

83

COMPANY:
FRANKENSTEIN!!!

(There is one final burst of lightning that strikes the tombstone and the candles all simultaneously go out, leaving the stage in complete darkness.)

Blackout.
Finis

CURTAIN CALL ORDER:
Genevans
Fritz, DeLacey
Alphonse, William
Henry, Justine
Elizabeth
Creature
Victor

About the Composer/Librettist

Michael Daniel was born and raised in Kailua-Kona, Hawaii. He started writing *Frankenstein*, his first musical, at the age of sixteen. He has also written the book, music and lyrics for the musical comedy *The Show Must Go On* and the musical revue *Staying and Getting Together*. He also collaborated as lyricist/co-composer with composer Leinad Ekim on the musicals *Sleepy Hollow* and *Alone: A Musical Dramedy*.

In addition to writing for the live stage, Michael has composed the musical scores for numerous short films, and the feature films *Blood Rush* (for which he won the 2012 Hollywood Investigator Tabloid Witch Award for Best Musical Soundtrack), and *Horror House*.

Michael attended the Berklee College of Music in Boston, Massachusetts, where he majored in Film Scoring, and he received his Master of Fine Arts in Film Music Composition from the University of North Carolina School of the Arts in Winston-Salem, North Carolina.

Michael currently resides in Anaheim, California, with his wife, Gina.

For more information about Michael and his musical works, visit http://michaeldaniel.net

www.ingramcontent.com/pod-product-compliance
Lightning Source LLC
Chambersburg PA
CBHW020513030426
42337CB00011B/364